D1266602

Library of Congress Cataloging-in-Publication Data

Watts, Barrie.
  Moth / Barrie Watts.
    p.   cm.—(Stopwatch)
    "First published by A & C Black ... adapted and published in the United
States in 1990 by Silver Burdett Press"—CIP t.p. verso.
    Includes index.
    Summary: Photographs help show the life cycle of the moth from the egg
and caterpillar stages to the moment it emerges from the cocoon as a flying
insect.
    1. Moths—Juvenile literature.   2. Moths—Life cycles—Juvenile
literature.   3. Luna moth—Juvenile literature.   [1. Moths.]
  I. Title.   II. Series: Stopwatch books.
  QL544.2.W38   1990   90-44863
  595.78'1—dc20   CIP
                                                                  AC

    ISBN 0-382-24218-1   ISBN 0-382-24220-3 (trade)

First published by A & C Black (Publishers) Limited
35 Bedford Row, London WC1R 4JH

© 1990 Barrie Watts

Adapted and published in the United States in 1991 by Silver Burdett Press,
Englewood Cliffs, New Jersey

Acknowledgements
The illustrations are by Helen Senior.
The publishers would like to thank Michael Chinery for his help and advice.

Filmset by August Filmsetting, Haydock, St. Helens.
Printed in Belgium by Proost International Book Production.

Moth

Barrie Watts

Silver Burdett Press • Englewood Cliffs, New Jersey

Here is a Moon moth.

Have you ever seen a moth flying around a light?

There are lots of different sorts of moths. They are different shapes and sizes. Look at the patterns on their wings.

Look at the photograph. This big moth is a Moon moth from North America. Moon moths will only fly when it is dark. You can see Moon moths in zoos and butterfly parks.

This book will tell you how a moth grows from a tiny egg.

915818

The moth looks for a mate.

The female Moon moth has eggs inside her.
She must find a mate before she can lay her eggs.
The female makes a special smell to attract a male.
Look at the small photograph.

This female uses a special part at the end of her body
to make the smell.

The male moth has feathery antennae on top of his head.
He uses the antennae to pick up the female's smell. Then
he follows the smell to find the female.

The moths mate.

The male and female moths mate at night. They mate for about four hours.

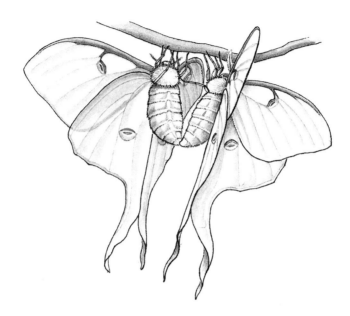

After the moths have mated, the male flies away to find another female.

Next evening, the female looks for a safe place to lay her eggs. She lays them in small groups on the leaves of a walnut tree. The female will lay up to 200 eggs. In the photograph the eggs look big. In real life each egg is as small as the top of a pin.

The eggs hatch.

Ten days later, small caterpillars eat their way out of the eggs. Each caterpillar is only as big as a grain of rice.

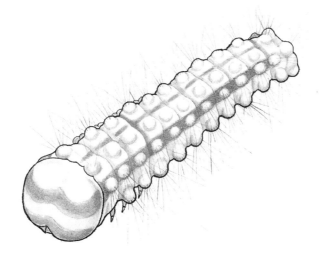

Look at the photograph. These young caterpillars have just hatched. Now they will crawl a long way from the egg shells. As soon as a tiny caterpillar has found a safe place under a leaf, it will start to eat.

The caterpillar changes its skin.

The caterpillar eats all the time. It grows very quickly and gets fatter.

As the caterpillar grows, its skin gets tighter.

Soon the caterpillar's skin starts to split. The caterpillar wriggles out of its old skin. A new skin has formed underneath. Look at the big photograph. Can you see the old skin left behind?

The caterpillar changes its skin five times before it is fully grown.

The caterpillar grows quickly.

Look at the big photograph. The caterpillar is using its strong jaws to chew a leaf. It eats several leaves every day.

The caterpillar's body is divided into thirteen segments. It uses its legs and feet to grip on to leaves.

The caterpillar will grow to be about 2$\frac{1}{2}$ inches long – that's about as long as your middle finger. Not all the caterpillars live to become this big. Many are eaten by other insects and birds.

The caterpillar makes a cocoon.

The caterpillar is now fully grown. It stops eating and finds a safe place high up in a tree. Then it starts to make a cocoon.

Look at the big photograph. The caterpillar makes sticky thread from a hole near its mouth. It starts to wind the thread round its body. The caterpillar pulls the leaf around the cocoon with the sticky thread.

When the cocoon is finished it is as big as a golf ball. It covers the caterpillar completely.

The caterpillar changes into a pupa.

Soon the outside of the cocoon becomes hard.
This cocoon has been cut in half. The caterpillar
rests inside.

After a week, the caterpillar's skin splits. Inside,
there is a pupa. Look at the big photograph. The pupa
has a hard skin. A moth is growing inside the pupa. Can
you see the dried-up caterpillar skin next to the pupa?

A moth comes out of the cocoon.

After three weeks, the moth is ready to come out.
It pushes from inside until the skin of the pupa splits.
Then it struggles out of the pupa.

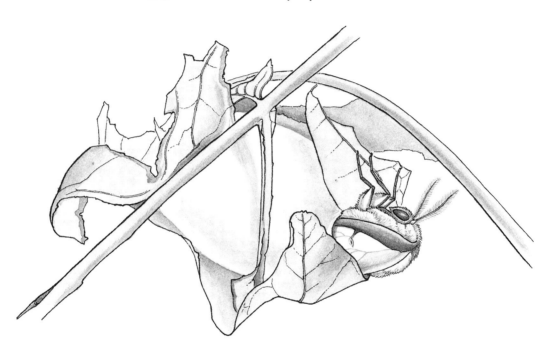

The moth makes a special juice to soften the cocoon.
Then the moth pushes its way out of the cocoon.

At first, the moth's wings are soft and crumpled. The
moth hangs from a leaf and waits for its wings to dry.

The moth's wings begin to dry.

After ten minutes the moth's wings have nearly doubled in size.

After twenty minutes the wings are full size.
They are almost dry. But the moth cannot fly yet.

When the moth's wings are dry, it opens them out.
Then it rests until nighttime.

The moth flies off to find a mate.

The moth's wings are dry. It is ready to fly for the first time. It flaps its wings up and down very quickly to warm up its muscles. Then the moth flies away.

Moon moths do not have mouths and they cannot eat. So they only live for about ten days. They must find a mate.

The male moth flies off as soon as it can. But the female moth sometimes stays and waits for a male to find her. What do you think will happen then?

Do you remember how the moth came from the egg?
See if you can tell the story in your own words.
You can use these pictures to help you.

1

2

4

5

3

6

Index

This index will help you to find some of the important words in this book.

You may be able to buy or find a moth caterpillar and watch it grow. Remember to give it fresh leaves every day.